# THE ART OF
# TIVAEVAE

## TE TUI NEI AU

*Te tui nei au i taku tivaevae*

*Ei rakei i to tatou kainga*

*E kara kura no to upoko*

*E kara renga no te tino*


*Te tavake no Havaiki mai*

*Kua moe ki runga*

*i taku tivaevae*


*I am sewing this quilt*

*to beautify our home*

*Red for the head*

*Gold for the body*


*The tropical bird from Havaiki*

*has fallen asleep upon my tivaevae*

KAURAKA KAURAKA
1990

# THE ART OF
# TIVAEVAE

### TRADITIONAL COOK ISLANDS QUILTING

LYNNSAY RONGOKEA   PHOTOGRAPHS BY JOHN DALEY

UNIVERSITY OF HAWAI'I PRESS
HONOLULU

*This book is dedicated to the many Cook Islands women I have met who constantly inspire me, and to my daughters Serena, Marie, Sarah, Charlotte and Bonita for the gift each of them brings to my life*

Published in North America by
University of Hawai'i Press
2840 Kolowalu Street
Honolulu, Hawai'i 96822

First published in New Zealand by Random House New Zealand
18 Poland Road, Glenfield, Auckland, New Zealand
www.randomhouse.co.nz

First published 2001
© 2001 Lynnsay Rongokea (text), John Daley (photographs)
The moral rights of the author and photographer have been asserted
ISBN 0-8248-2502-0

Design and production: Inhouse Design
Printed in Singapore

ACKNOWLEDGEMENTS

I again express my heartfelt thanks to all the women and members of my family who so generously invited John Daley and me into their homes, shared their stories and allowed photographs to be taken of themselves and their tivaevae for the book. Special thanks to: Vereara Maeva, one very remarkable woman; Tokerau Munro and members of her vaine-tini; Esther Katu and her family for arranging the haircutting scene, and young Mathew Suafa'i Ross Toleafoa for his cooperation and patience; and Parau Taruia.

For this book in which the text and photography carry equal weight, the work of the photographer was of importance and I thank John Daley for his shared vision and phenomenal dedication to this project. Thanks also to Jane Connor of Random House for the conviction that risks are worth it.

I acknowledge the love, support and friendship of my daughters: Marie, who helped me to refocus to complete this project; Serena for assisting with text; Sarah, Charlotte and Bonita for the phone calls that lifted my spirit. Also my sister Malina Cleary for her enthusiastic encouragement and Kim Stanford-Smith for the loving friendship. I'm grateful for the unfailing help and emotional support of my extended family: Tearii Halligan, Connie and Arthur, Jaqueline and Tainui, Tutu Koteka, Maria Ngaputa Heather, Emily Simiona, Nooroa Teina, Ota Joseph and Elizabeth Araiti Ponga. Rangi Moekaa has validated my work by agreeing to write the foreword, and I acknowledge the late Kauraka Kauraka for his special poems.

I thank sincerely the following people for their help and support given in many ways: Michael Gifkins, Tim Tepaki, Jim Gosselin, Teararoa Mani, Josephine Lockington, Bishop Leamy, Niki Rattle, Madeline Metcalfe, Pai Mataroa, Frances Apera, Sonny Williams, Ewan Smith of Air Rarotonga, Gerda Leenards, Lindsay Missen, Kobi Bosshard, Air New Zealand (C.I.s) and those on the outer islands who extended their hospitality to us.

Finally, from the past I acknowledge my mother, Mary Rongokea, the instigator of this project, a superb seamstress who inspired me to come to know the many pleasures of working with fibre and fabric, passed on to her granddaughters Sarah and Bonita.

# CONTENTS

6

*Tivaevae tataura by Tara Ngataua*

# FOREWORD

I am happy and delighted with the privilege and honour given to me to provide the foreword to this illuminative collection of not only artistic, creative and decorative art forms, but functional as well. For me, the intricacies and aesthetic qualities of the *tïvaevae* portray and reflect the vibrant threads and nuances of our Cook Islands culture. The womenfolk have not only taken the art of *tïvaevae making* to the pinnacle of excellence, but subconsciously expressed their innermost feelings of love and appreciation for their environments. They are heartily congratulated and commended.

Commendations are also due to the author for her inspiration, integrity and skilful coordination of unique experiences, knowledge and practical skills of the artisans. It would be well for those aspiring to these accomplishments to take heed of the message and put it to use. As an old, wise and greyhaired *mämä* would often remind a recalcitrant daughter:

*Paea i Ra`imanava*
*Manava, manava, manava!*

*Promulgated at Ra'imanava*
*Absorb the knowledge; persevere and practise it!*

Knowledge and skills are maintained through practice.

Kia orana 'e kia manuia
Rangitukua Moeka`a
Centre for Pacific Studies, University of Auckland

*Tivaevae manu by Tutai Cameron*

# INTRODUCTION

*For centuries the women of the South Pacific have made a unique contribution to customary art forms, translating cultural themes and values into symbolic visual interpretations of the world around them and their own proud place within it.*

Nowhere is this more true than among the women of the Cook Islands. This group of fifteen islands lies in the South Pacific ocean virtually in the centre of the Polynesian triangle, south of Hawaii, flanked to the west by Tonga and Samoa and to the east by French Polynesia, and to the south by Aotearoa (New Zealand). The Cook Islands are made up of the Southern and Northern Groups, with a total land area of 240 square kilometres, spread over two million square kilometres of ocean. The Southern group includes Rarotonga, Aitutaki, Atiu, Mitiaro, Mauke and Mangaia, Manuae and Takutea. The Northern Group consists mainly of atolls including Penrhyn, Rakahanga, Manihiki, Pukapuka, Nassau, Suwarrow and Palmerston. The indigenous population of the Cook Islands is Polynesian and has strong historical links with other Polynesians in the region.

The last hundred years have witnessed exciting developments in the forms and styles of artistic expression of the women of the Cook Islands, particularly in needlework and especially in tivaevae. There is no written record of how or when the sewing of tivaevae was introduced to the Cook Islands. Some say the wives of the London Missionary Society missionaries, who arrived here in 1821, might have taught it; others hold that it was learned from the Tahitian missionaries who helped introduce Christianity to the Cook Islands. In 1895, for instance, three Catholic nuns (one Irish, two French) came to Rarotonga from Tahiti and taught quilting, embroidery, needlework, sewing, crochet and tatting at the local Catholic school. Whatever its origin, tivaevae slipped easily and permanently into the daily and ceremonial life of Cook Islands society. Both the

*Plants are used as adornments for dance costumes*

patterns that have developed and the methods by which tivaevae are put together are distinctly Cook Islands.

Within the last few decades needlework has reached new heights of excellence. Building upon traditional themes and styles, the women have subtly incorporated new concepts and designs into their creations, reflecting the changing contemporary world in which they play such a critical role. At the same time they have steadily maintained and indeed improved the technical quality and precision of their work, providing a foundation from which further creative work in tivaevae making can develop.

Since its introduction to the Cook Islands, tivaevae making has become a social activity in which groups of women in the local communities join together to cut and sew the designs. In the earlier days, when tere parties [visitors or travellers] visited the different islands, gifts of tivaevae would be presented to hosts, and as women travelled between Rarotonga, the outer islands and Tahiti, they shared their designs and skills.

Tivaevae patterns are inspired by and reflect the environment of the Cook Islands. Flowers and plants, such an important part of the Cook Islands lifestyle and customs, form the basis of virtually all tivaevae designs. In addition they are used in traditional medicines, as decorations for ceremonies and functions, and as adornments for dance costumes; they are given in the spirit of love and friendship to family, friends and visitors as an ei kaki [a garland of flowers placed around the neck and shoulders] followed by an embrace; and are worn by some as part of everyday dress with a flower behind the ear (which used to signify marital status or availability) or as an ei katu [a circular head crown]. Much thought is put into colour combinations and contrasts in the designs, and some women have their own interpretations of how colour should be used. In the outer islands it is said the women experiment more often with different colours, creating, for example, blue roses and purple hibiscus, much to the disgust of those who think the 'proper' colour of the flower should be used.

The value of tivaevae is more than just decorative. The images of the colour and life of the local environment combine with the care with which each tivaevae is sewn, the love with which they are given as gifts, as well as their decorative role at public ceremonies and family occasions to give tivaevae a wider social and cultural meaning. Women who find the time to be creative—outside caring for their families, household chores, planting and income-earning jobs —make tivaevae. Most women, after learning how to sew at home or at school, teach themselves to make tivaevae by observing other women and then practising what they have learned. Nowadays the craft is not as widely practised among the younger generation as it once was, with other

more modern interests taking the place of tivaevae making. Tivaevae making continues to be a community-centred activity (although some women prefer to work alone), with women in the different villages sewing their tivaevae in vaine-tini [women's groups]. Working in these groups, the women eat together, sing, and talk about themselves, their families and their community.

Most women know how to cut and sew tivaevae, but only a few women are expert in the art of designing, as well as cutting and sewing. Such women have attained the status of a taunga [a person who is highly skilled in any art]. The women may not always be able to say where a particular idea for a pattern has come from, but many find inspiration in their own vision of their environment, drawing an interpretation of what they see directly onto the fabric, or onto paper, lino, or a large plastic sheet before transferring it to the fabric. With a taorei [patchwork design] the pattern is coloured onto a woven pandanus mat or graph paper.

Designs of a particular taunga are usually recognisable and are sometimes copied (although no two tivaevae are the same; the maker may repeat the pattern but change the colour combination and slightly alter part of the design). Some women are not willing for anyone outside the family to copy their designs, however most taunga feel quite honoured when others copy their patterns once the tivaevae is finished and exhibited. It would be annoying only if a woman claimed a pattern to be her own.

A number of women who sew tivaevae are superstitious and won't use designs of the peacock, mermaid and other marine life as it may bring bad luck. Others believe they would lose their ability to design and sew if they were to sell their tivaevae. Most

*Vaine-tini groups around the island hold exhibitions or shows of tivaevae*

are not interested in selling their work because of the attachment they feel towards it; there is also the fear that they might not be able to make another one like it.

Women sew tivaevae for their own enjoyment. They are usually made for family members but they may be given away outside the family. They are often presented to visiting dignitaries and church ministers; when a church minister or a diplomat begins a new term or when their term comes to an end, the vainetini group in the village will sew tivaevae for the minister or diplomat and his wife. Different vaine-tini groups around the island hold exhibitions or shows of tivaevae every year and at the Cook Islands National Council of Women's biannual conference. Here the islands by government health inspectors and welfare women. Begun in 1946 by Sir Thomas Davis, the doctor in charge of medical services at the time, the six-monthly tutaka inspections became an important social event. Women made tivaevae, pillowcases, cushion covers, crocheted tablecloths and doilies to be displayed in their homes during the inspection. The tutaka continues to be a significant event, but with improved health awareness and modern utilities, homes on Rarotonga are now inspected only on the outside. On the outer islands, however, the tutaka is still considered an occasion worth creative preparation.

The beautifully crafted tivaevae are an integral part of special occasions on the islands. At baptisms, the birth of a child, weddings, funerals or haircutting ceremonies tivaevae are used for decoration as well as given away. New tivaevae are made and old tivaevae are taken out of the wooden chests, plastic bags and cupboards in which they're kept, and aired on the clothesline before being displayed on walls, draped over chairs or spread across beds. It is not unusual for

tivaevae to be handed down through many generations, and not be used but be stored for many years and taken out only when a close family member dies.

Tivaevae are sought-after gifts at weddings. An oora [presentation of gifts] may be performed in which the bride traditionally presents gifts to her husband, or gifts are presented to both, including tivaevae that she and sometimes other members of her family or close family friends have sewn. After the marriage ceremony, the couple is seated on chairs covered with tivaevae, and guests will dance up to them to the rhythm of the drumbeat and present them with tivaevae, other gifts and money. Tivaevae are used also to decorate the area around the main table.

*Pakotianga rauru—Mathew Suafa'i Ross Toleafoa*

At funerals tivaevae are used to cover the bed if the body is brought home prior to burial. A woven pandanus mat or a tivaevae sometimes lines the grave or casket, or the tivaevae may be draped over the casket and buried with the family member.

The pakotianga rauru is a traditional ceremony still practised by some Cook Islanders during which boys aged between five and twenty-one have their first haircut. Invitations are sent out to family and close friends, and each will attend the ceremony to cut a lock of hair. The boy's hair, uncut since birth, is plaited, or locks taken and tied with ribbons and then cut. The tivaevae are presented as gifts as well as being used to decorate the walls and draped over the chair on which the boy sits. In Nga-pu-toru, the islands of Atiu, Mitiaro and Mauke, haircutting is considered to be a name-giving celebration where the first-born male child has been named after or by a grandparent, or after someone from past generations who holds the respect of the clan, for example a chief. There is a myth that to cut a boy's hair while he is less than one

year would lead to the child having a speech impediment. On Rarotonga some mothers don't cut their son's hair from birth because they consider it too beautiful to cut.

For Cook Islanders the value of tivaevae is not measured in terms of material worth—although, considering the price of materials and the time and care the women devote to their creations, that worth is high. Tivaevae are valuable because they reflect so many aspects of the community—the plants, life and colour of the environment; the relationships among the women who sew the tivaevae; the relationships between the people who have given and received tivaevae as gifts; and the links between past and present-day Cook Islands society.

# HOW TIVAEVAE ARE MADE

There are two basic methods of sewing tivaevae: patchwork, also known as piecework, and appliqué. These two methods are used to make up the four different styles: tivaevae taorei (piecework/patchwork), tivaevae manu (appliqué), tivaevae tataura (appliqué with embroidery) and tivaevae tuitui tataura (embroidered squares of fabric joined together with either crocheting or with lace borders). It can take from one week to two years or more to complete a tivaevae, depending on the intricacy of the design, the time spent on sewing and the number of women working on it.

*Tivaevae taorei* are small pieced or patchwork bedspreads made from small pieces of coloured cotton fabric (the size of a thumbnail or about an inch wide) cut into shapes—squares, hexagons, diamonds and triangles. Four or more colours are used to create an effective design forming a pattern. It is estimated it takes about 15,000 squares to make a double-bed cover and up to 56,000 to make a king-size cover. It is normally sewn by a group of four to eight women

*Sewing a tivaevae taorei*

and they will often work on a tivaevae for each member of their group. The taorei technique allows for many intricate geometric design variations through the use of colour combinations, creating popular designs of flowers (chrysanthemums, roses, lilies), the turtle, the crown and the Star of David. Women would sometimes use old cotton dresses and shirts to make their taorei.

Once the pattern of a taorei has been designed in colour, either on a pandanus mat or piece of graph paper, a sample corner is prepared to show the women the order of colours. When the vaine-tini meets, the woman who has designed the pattern will instruct the others on tearing and cutting the fabric into small squares or whatever the shape may be. When all the fabric has been cut, the women equip themselves with needle, thread and their small pieces of fabric in front of them, and the designer proceeds to call out the order of colours, e.g. two blue, four red, ten green. The women each sew the coloured squares of material onto a length of thread as she calls, separating each

colour change with a coloured square not used in the overall design. It is crucial the women listen carefully and thread the correct number of coloured squares because an error in the order of colours will throw the whole pattern out. After all the fabric has been sewn onto the threads, each woman will start sewing her section of the tivaevae, guided by her small sample. When they have each completed their sections, they come together again and the sections are laid on the floor to make sure they fit before they are sewn up. If the coloured squares have been correctly threaded, the pattern will work out. If not, it is a very time-consuming job to correct, and usually only the designer of the tivaevae taorei can identify where the error is and correct it. The top will then be sewn onto a piece of backing material, which is folded and sewn down to cover the raw edges to complete the tivaevae.

*Tivaevae manu* are appliquéd bedspreads made using two contrasting colours of cotton fabric, one for the pattern and one for the background. Some women

*A template made of lino, plastic or paper is used to trace the design onto the fabric*

nowadays use two different coloured sheets. In the early days these tivaevae were always made using red blue or green on white. The top layer is folded into four. The design may be drawn straight onto the fabric, or a template made of lino, plastic or paper is used to trace the design onto the fabric before it is cut out. The cutout fabric is then opened out, tacked and sewn onto the background material using an invisible stitch, sometimes it is then embroidered around the edges of the pattern with a zigzag stitch.

*Tivaevae tuitui tataura* (appliqué and embroidery) bedspreads are made using three or more coloured fabrics, then embroidered with variegated pearl cotton using a combination of stitches on different parts of the pattern. Stitches include featherstitch, fly stitch, stem stitch, chain stitch, long and short stitch, padded satin stitch, seed stitch and others. There are two different ways of sewing a tivaevae tataura. In one, the pattern shapes are cut out on fabric then tacked and sewn onto the backing sheet (the same steps as for the tivaevae manu), then embroidered. The sewing on the reverse is often so neat that it could be used in reverse. In the second method, once the shapes of coloured fabric have been cut, the embroidery is done first before being tacked and sewn onto the backing material, then the embroidery around the edges is completed. The embroidery stitching is a very important feature of this tivaevae, incorporating the colour combinations of both the embroidery cotton and the fabric. The women use the stitching as an artist uses his paints.

*Tivaevae tuitui tataura* are embroidered squares of material (the size of a small cushion cover), which are crocheted together before being sewn onto a backing sheet. In Manihiki the women sew the pieces together using lace instead of crocheting.

*Tivaevae manu by Ani Maoate*

*Tivaevae tataura by Mareta Matamua*

*Tivaevae taorei by Taarouru Apera*

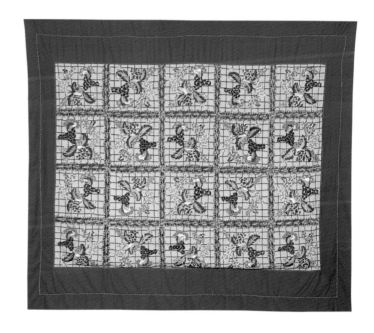

*Tivaevae tuitui tataura by Parau Taruia*

# TAAROURU APERA

*My grandmother sewed and crocheted—she was good at everything—and wouldn't allow us kids to touch her sewing. I always remember my mother sewing. She was left-handed and people didn't want to learn off a left-handed person because it was hard to follow the stitches.*

I learned to sew in the 1970s. I had a friend who was good at sewing and always carried her sewing around with her. I asked her to teach me and she taught me some stitches. I sewed a tablecloth then pillowslips and cushions before making my first tivaevae. When my mother died, I wrapped that tivaevae around her coffin. I've still got the tablecloths and pillowslips.

I learned to sew tivaevae by joining a group. I've cut about four tivaevae so far. I enjoy sewing tivaevae tataura because I like the different embroidery stitches, and I've just finished my first tivaevae taorei.

I sew tivaevae by myself and I also work with a group. We all decide on which pattern we are going to sew, one woman cuts the pattern, then the whole group sews it together. I enjoy sewing flowers—what else is there to sew? My favourite colours are a mixture of light and dark. I have two daughters. At present, they're not interested in sewing.

*Women use stitching as an artist uses paints*

M A T I R I T A (CHRYSANTHEMUM) *Tivaevae manu*

R O T I  (ROSE)  *Tivaevae tataura*

# TUNGANE CAMERON

*When I was about eighteen my mother taught me how to sew. That mother of mine, she's a very clever woman. She knows how to cut and sew dresses and pants, and how to cut the pattern for the tivaevae manu, tataura, taorei and the paka onu. But the women of today don't really want to sew a taorei because you have to cut it small and it takes a long time to sew.*

I taught my girls how to cut dresses, pants and shirts, but they don't know how to cut tivaevae. Their minds are not on tivaevae.

Some of our patterns are from Tahiti. I like to sew flower patterns. I've made tivaevae that are orchids, lilies, hibiscus and pineapples. We've called the pattern on one of the tivaevae I've made 'tiare ora varu'—at eight o'clock the flower opens—that's how I see it.

I have ten daughters and two boys. All the girls know how to sew but they don't know how to cut tivaevae. I think they'll learn how to. I cut the pattern and my daughter sews. I've got plenty of tivaevae because my daughters help me to sew them.

TIARE ORA VARU (EIGHT O'CLOCK FLOWER) *Tivaevae tataura*

R I R I   V A I   (WATER LILY)   *Tivaevae tataura*

# AMIRIA DAVEY

*I have eleven children—five boys and six girls. I am part Hawaiian, Tahitian, English and Aitutakian. I'm from a family of fourteen, seven boys and seven girls. I am the third child in my family. I'm involved with vaine-tini, sports, child welfare, Sunday School, Girls' Brigade, and youth organisations. My hobbies are singing, fishing, planting, story-writing and story-telling, sewing, embroidery and weaving.*

Sewing and embroidery run in the family. My grandmother, Mahina, was the granddaughter of Prince John William Kanoa of Puna, Hawaii. She was an expert in weaving, embroidery and knitting. My mother was an expert in weaving and embroidery.

I learned patchwork when I was twelve years old. I used to watch my mother sewing and she would give me the small squares of her tivaevae to tack together. At secondary school we were taught sewing and embroidery stitches on plain squares of material. Then we started sewing handkerchiefs and we could do embroidery stitches on them. During that time we were also shown how to cut out patterns on paper for sewing dresses, and flowers for embroidery work that we used for cushions.

# AMIRIA DAVEY

*I became more creative and tried other patterns like breadfruit*

Because I learned how to cut out patterns at school, I was able to cut them out. My first patterns were flowers, then I became more creative and tried other patterns like breadfruit, pineapples, dolphins, birds, crabs and mermaids. I draw my patterns on paper first, then I fold the material and cut out my pattern. Sometimes I cut out patterns and stitch them to a single bed sheet to make up a tivaevae. Two of my daughters are good at cutting out their own patterns and sewing clothes and tivaevae. They would watch me when I cut out patterns and then just follow what I was doing. They learned sewing at school but I taught them how to cut and sew tivaevae. They sew tivaevae manu and make embroidered pillowcases to match.

M E R I O (MERMAID) *Tivaevae tataura*

# RANGI ENOKA

*I was twenty years old when I first tried to make my own tivaevae. In those days we learned by watching other women. I belonged to a vaine-tini group in Avatiu—my mother-in-law was the president. I watched my mother-in-law and the other women making their own tivaevae, then I'd come back home and make my own; that's how I learned to sew.*

There were about six women in the group. We'd meet every three weeks to work on a taorei. We sung ute [lively songs] to make ourselves happy and the women would cook a kaikai [meal]. We would buy our own material, then it would take us about two or three weeks to make the taorei, working on it every day.

For the tivaevae taorei, once we decided on the pattern, we'd tear the material into strips and cut it into small squares, diamonds or triangles. We would count the colours to make up the pattern then thread the squares or whatever onto a piece of cotton. Everyone would have a corner to sew and when each woman had finished her corner, we'd sew them together to make up the tivaevae. Once that was done, the pattern would be sewn onto a backing sheet.

We used to take the tivaevae taorei down to the beach on a hot day and stretch it out. It would take about four to six women to pull it straight before laying it onto the sand, the top side turned down,

*We used to take the tivaevae taorei down to the beach on a hot day and stretch it out*

33

# RANGIENOKA

with stones around the edges. We'd sprinkle a little cold water over it and when it dried it would be nice and straight.

I started sewing tivaevae taorei and, later, I wanted to sew tivaevae manu. I wasn't very good to begin with but I kept trying. Finally, I finished my tivaevae. Now I know that it is not an impossible task once you put your mind to it. In those days, we didn't have much money but it cost one pound six shillings a yard [for material] and a tivaevae manu takes five yards of material for the top and seven yards for the back. One problem was finding a person to cut the tivaevae. Before I learned how to do it, I used to take my material to Aihao. He lived in town and he'd cut all our tivaevae for us. I paid him two pounds to cut mine. It was hard work to find that money. Sometimes he would take a long time and he would say it was because it was hard work. I used to get tired of waiting

for him and it was expensive so I decided to cut my own tivaevae. The first one wasn't very good but my second tivaevae was good. The first time, I drew a flower on paper and then afterwards I drew straight onto the material, which was easier. When I had cut out my pattern, I couldn't wait to finish sewing to see how it would turn out. I use my patterns more than once, but I use a different colour material. I like roses and tiare maori. When I learned how to cut tivaevae, women came to me to cut theirs. They wanted to pay me but I was too ashamed to take their money, so I taught some of them and then they knew how to do it themselves. I taught three of my daughters how to sew tivaevae.

I feel sorry when I give my tivaevae away. I worry that maybe I can't make another one like that. I don't sell my tivaevae because they're too hard to make. I just give them to my children and my grandchildren.

MATIRITA (CHRYSANTHEMUM) *Tivaevae tataura*

# NORMA IRO

*I started sewing when I went to school. I was interested because my mother sewed and did needlework. My mother liked that kind of work, making things for her house to make it look nice. I've still got a lot of her sewing.*

When I first started to sew tivaevae, I would go to my mother-in-law and tell her what pattern I had in my mind and she would cut it out for me. Sometimes I would cut out the flowers and ask her to cut out the pattern for the leaves. That's how I learned to cut tivaevae, by watching her.

I'm very fussy about the way I sew my work and choosing the colours for a pattern. If it's a hard pattern, it takes me a long time to sew—about two to three years. I take care in sewing and finishing a tivaevae, making sure my stitches are neat and even. Sometimes I get tired of sewing the same tivaevae so I start a different one and could work on two or three at different times.

I spend time with my granddaughter and in my garden where I get ideas for patterns for my tivaevae, like the orchids and puru-akari tivaevae. I grow orchids and anthuriums in pots using puru-akari (husk of the coconut after removal from the nut) instead of soil.

*I grow orchids and anthuriums in pots using puru-akari (husk of the coconut after removal from the nut) instead of soil*

37

ORCHIDS AND PURU-AKARI (BROWN COCONUT HUSK) *Tivaevae tataura*

ANTHURIUMS  *Tivaevae tataura*

# POKO KAPI

*I was born in Atiu. When I was sixteen I came to live in Rarotonga with my brother. One of the ladies at school taught me embroidery on a pillowcase, but I didn't finish it because I wasn't really interested and couldn't be bothered.*

When I was at school I was taught how to sew. We made pillowcases and that's how I learned to hold the needle and cotton. I used to watch my grandmother sewing but she never taught me. I wasn't really interested then, but in my mind I thought I would try one day. My mother passed away when I was very young so I don't know much about her. Some people say she could sew tivaevae, and my grandmother certainly could.

After many years of watching old ladies sew, my mind was always on tivaevae but the problem was that I didn't know how to cut the patterns. I was anxious to learn but there was no one to help me. I kept saying to myself, one day I will learn. I used to pay a friend of mine to cut them. I was preparing for my eldest daughter's wedding and I said to myself, 'I'm wasting a lot of money getting this lady to cut my tivaevae, but I have to pay her because I don't know how to do it myself.'

41

I took a trip to New Zealand because my sister is there and is one of the tutors for a group sewing tivaevae in the town where she lives. So I went there and begged her to help me. I asked her to teach me.

She would draw the pattern on a piece of paper, so I traced it and she taught me how to fold the tivaevae and cut it following the lines. When I'd finished cutting, she showed me how to spread it and I followed her instructions. I cut out the pattern and spread it out on the backing with my sister watching me. When I made a mistake she corrected me—that's how I learned. I still have the first tivaevae I cut at home. Now I help other women cut and design their tivaevae.

I love drawing flowers. I draw the pattern on the paper, lay it on the material and cut it out. I like bright colours: reds and blues. I sew tivaevae manu, tivaevae tataura, tivaevae karakara. I've made one tivaevae taorei but it's very old. I sew tivaevae for my children. I don't mind cutting for family but I get scared to cut for anyone else in case I make a mistake—the material is too expensive.

The most difficult part of the tivaevae is cutting the pattern and laying it out on the backing material. Once the pattern is laid out, it is tacked to the backing material ready to be stitched by hand or embroidered. But now I am just happy that I know how to design and cut out patterns.

M O R I   T A U T A U   (HANGING LANTERN)  *Tivaevae manu*

R I R I  V A I  (WATER LILY) *Tivaevae tataura*

K A U T E  (HIBISCUS)  *Tivaevae tataura*

TIARE MAORI (GARDENIA) *Tivaevae manu*

# VEREARA MAEVA

*I was born and raised on the island of Aitutaki by my grandparents and my Aunty Ngaupoko (my birth mother's sister), whom I believed to be my real mother. I was the first grandchild in my grandfather Teariki Monga's family and the eldest in a family of seven, whom I later learned about.*

My grandfather, Teariki Monga, was a very dignified orator, a song writer, a musician and entertainer, knowledgeable in culture and the performing arts. He held traditional titles in all the four Ariki families on Aitutaki—Tamatoa, Vaeruarangi, Teurukura and Manaraingi Ariki.

My grandmother, Te Kauvai Tatira, was a descendant of Paenui Rangatira, under Tinomana Ariki of Arorangi, with Aitutaki, Rarotonga and Mangaian blood connections. She taught me to sew tivaevae and to do embroidery, sewing, weaving and other handwork. My feeding mother, Ngaupoko Teariki Monga, was also skilled at sewing, cooking and embroidery.

These were the three very important people in my childhood, very loving and caring, from whom I inherited the many life- skills of womanhood and my culture, of which I am very proud. My only regret is that they are no longer around today to enjoy the fruit of their upbringing.

*Tivaevae tuitui tataura are crocheted together*

49

# VEREARAMAEVA

From when I was about five years old, I'd sit around with my grandmother, my aunty and her women friends each time they got together to do their women's work—be it tivaevae making, embroidery, plaiting mats, weaving kikau baskets or even singing. They would often meet at our house once a week, mostly to make tivaevae. I developed an interest in practically everything that they were doing. They would sing ute, imene tuki and even gossip, and I always enjoyed listening to them and would sing along with them. Sometimes my grandmother would make me dance for them and they would give me lollies and other nice things for my dancing.

I would watch my grandmother show them the basics of tivaevae making. She was quite artistic in that she was able to do freehand drawing of patterns straight on to the material ready for cutting. She wouldn't cut the tivaevae for them but would encourage the women to try and cut it themselves so they could learn fast. I think I have taken after her in that respect.

I use to help my grandmother with her tivaevae taorei, I'd help her tear the material into long strips and cut them into small squares. She'd copy patterns from old taorei that had been given to her by her own grandmother. It was quite a complicated process, counting the pieces and putting colours together to work out the pattern, and it required a lot of time, patience, commitment and perseverance. It takes much longer to prepare and sew a taorei as it is a much more complicated process than the other types of tivaevae.

It must have been very frustrating for my grandmother and my feeding mother as each time they left their work to attend to something else, I would have a try, believing that I could do it just as well as they did. Often I'd spoil their nice work, but they never spanked me. They were always happy to see me learning to do things and they helped me a lot.

M A T I R I T A (CHRYSANTHEMUM) *Tivaevae taorei*

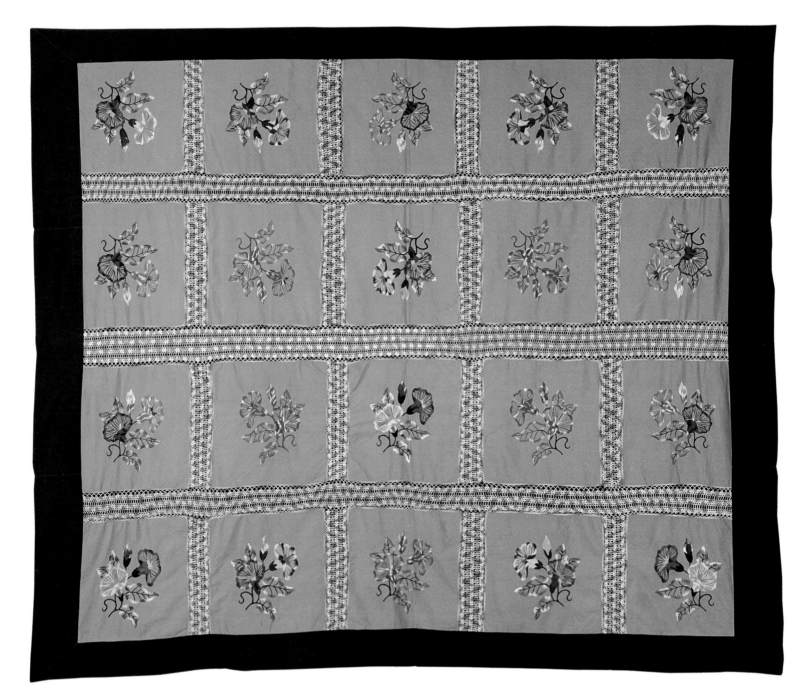

MIXED FLOWERS *Tivaevae tuitui tataura*

# VEREARaMAEVA

When I could afford it, I bought some more material and cut my first tivaevae manu to match the pillow covers. It took me almost six months, in between my study and other things, to complete. I won a prize for it during the village tutaka. I'd covered my bed with my tivaevae and pillow covers. I remembered this very special occasion because my grandma and my feeding mother came to Rarotonga to join the celebration of my sixteenth birthday. When I was twenty-one, my grandmother gave me three tivaevae for my birthday. She died not long after. One of them was a taorei. Unfortunately it was given away by mistake to a friend. How I wished I could swap that tivaevae back with another of my own creations.

In later years, as I acquired and improved my skills in tivaevae making and other needlecraft, I started following other older women to women's meetings to learn more about tivaevae making, which was the most common activity that women would do in their own small groups. In the many women's groups that I have joined or established over the years, during my travels with my family around the Cook Islands, I have tried to help other women in their quest to learn and make things for their families. In most cases, it has always been tivaevae that women were interested in making. It has been quite difficult in the outer islands, especially choosing the right material and cotton for the tivaevae. Women made do with what they could get and in most cases, the colours did not suit the pattern, but women would just use colours out of the ordinary. Somehow it didn't matter at all, as long as they were able to learn and make their own tivaevae, and they would feel very happy and proud of their effort.

I can't help feeling sad about the fact that our young girls today don't seem to care or understand the value of our tivaevae, nor have the interest to learn the skills. It will be a great loss to our culture if we don't wake up now and try and save this unique and priceless gift of wisdom from our grandmothers, our mothers and the Almighty. 'Take heed of the wisdom of the "old" for thine is the joy and pride of belonging and owning an identity of being a true Cook Islands Woman'.

# maretaMATAMUA

*I'm now eighty-one years old. The mother who gave birth to me, her name was Ani, she worked as a nurse up at the hospital. I was brought up by my aunty Moari. My aunty and myself used to sew together—she was the one who showed me how to sew tivaevae.*

My mother didn't know. I only have one daughter, Esther. I've shown her how to sew and cut tivaevae and we've made many together. I've brought my grandchildren up and I've taught my granddaughter Ani to sew and now my great-granddaughter Nastashjia. We all live together.

I learned how to sew at the Arorangi School, in grade six or seven. The teacher at the time was Mr Walker and his wife, they were papaa. The girls in the class would go to their house after school and we'd learn how to sew. First time sewing, I started learning to sew an embroidered tablecloth with stem stitch, daisy stitch and button hole stitch. When we finished sewing our tablecloths we would sell them for money for the school.

I really started sewing tivaevae after I got married. We lived with my aunty for a while before we moved to look after the girls at the SDA school. When we got married I had two tivaevae but we didn't have an

*Mareta and great-granddaughter Nastashjia*

55

# mareta MATAMUA

oora. It was a tivaevae manu, a yellow one. I didn't cut it, my aunty cut it, and we both stitched it onto the backing material and then I sewed it by myself. I kept it and used it until it was ngaengae [torn and tattered]. My second one was a taorei. I sewed this one with my aunty, and some of the ladies from our group. It was a star pattern. With the taorei I don't know how to make my own pattern. Usually it's one mama in the group who knows how to draw the pattern for the taorei. In the olden days the women took the tivaevae taorei down to the beach and spread it on the white sand, with the right side down. Two or three women would pull each corner and put stones on the corners, sprinkle it with water and leave it in the sun to straighten. Then you see the mistakes and untidy stitches, and they would tack and fix the areas that were not right then take it home and sew it onto the backing material. You can see when hanging a

tivaevae if it's nice and straight because it falls nicely; some tivaevae when hanging are lopsided. Sometimes a mistake can be made in the taorei when a woman has missed a colour. You find out when the group brings their half to put together and it's hard to fix.

I really wanted to know how to make tivaevae by myself, because it's very hard to go and ask someone to show you how to cut one or to cut it for you because you have to pay them a couple of hundred dollars. So I got brown paper and drew a flower. It started with a small flower, which got bigger and bigger. When I finished drawing I cut it out and put it on the folded material to trace, then cut it out, tacked it on to the backing spread out on the floor and then sewed. I can make tivaevae manu and tivaevae tataura. I draw my own patterns. If I like a flower, I'll make that flower. I like sewing with all colours. In the old days you could buy good-quality cotton material of all different colours and the dye didn't run, not like today, not the same quality.

When someone dies, there goes a tivaevae. When my mother and my aunty died, I covered them with two tivaevae. If I die, it's up to my children to decide what they want to do with the tivaevae.

*Tivaevae taorei*

# ESTHER KATU

I'm an only child. I have five children, three boys and two girls, but I only brought up my second child, my son Michael. The other four—Ani, Taimata, Edmond and Mareta—were brought up by my parents. We're a very close family and in between our travels—living overseas or on the outer islands—we've continued living together as an extended family. Since my father died a few years ago, it's been my husband, my mother, my daughter and the grandchildren.

When I was young my parents looked after the boarders at the SDA School. My father was a printer and my mother took care of the girls. I was about fourteen when mum taught me to sew an embroidery pillowslip. She used to make us all sit down and sew. She would tell us, 'If you don't learn to sew, what are you going to do when you grow up'. She was very strict with the girls and each girl had a pillowslip which she had to finish.

In 1964 when I got married my mother sewed everything. My husband was from Aitutaki, and when Aitutakian people get married—if you're the woman you're the one that's going to oora your husband. But when we got married it wasn't really an oora, they just put all the gifts together at once: the tivaevae, the mats, the cushions, etc—from my mother for me to give to my husband. My mother used to say, if you can't sew, your boyfriend won't like you.

It was only after I got married that I really started sewing. I had always wanted to sew a taorei. My very first tivaevae was a frangipani, and a friend's son was getting married so I gave it to him. I started cutting by watching my mother cut. I wanted to be able to do the cutting too because if there's no one to cut the pattern for you, you may as well learn to do it yourself. I have to have a pattern to start with. I can't draw a pattern freehand.

59

KAUTE (HIBISCUS) *Tivaevae taorei*

# MARETAMATAMUA

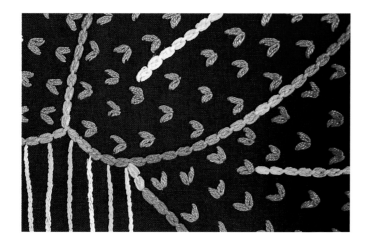

We store our tivaevae in the glory box and bring them out for the tutaka or when somebody's coming home. My husband used to say: 'How come I never get to use any of the tivaevae? When there's somebody coming home you put them on the beds, but when I'm home you don't put them on the bed for me'. I don't like putting the taorei on the beds here because it's too hot.

I'm a member of DORCAS and the Cook Islands National Council of Women, of which I've been a past president. When we have our biannual conference, we have a big tivaevae exhibition/competition. The women have a couple of years to prepare tivaevae for it and we have trophies and monetary prizes. We select judges from the community and we number the tivaevae so they don't know who they belong to. The tivaevae is judged on the sewing, pattern, the way they put the colours together and the material. In DORCAS a church organisation, in our village we

meet once a month, to study the Bible, visit people at home who may be sick, visit the prisons, visit families that may need help, and sometimes for a break we might sew tivaevae.

When my son Michael was two years old, my mother had made a tivaevae with a pansy pattern. He asked my mother who this tivaevae belonged to. He loved it and she put it away for him for when he grew up. When he got married a couple of years ago, it took us about six months to sew him ten tivaevae, taorei, manu, tataura. I was working at the time and during my morning/lunch/afternoon breaks and any spare time I had I would sew. He had an oora at his wedding and was presented with a total of twenty-four tivaevae, sixteen from my mother and I, and the rest from my family. You know it's not supposed to be the boys who bring the things to the marriage, it's you as a woman who takes gifts for your husband, but I didn't care. I love my son very much and was happy to do this for him. I was happy that I made those tivaevae myself.

My mother and I have worked on many tivaevae together. We've worked on a taorei with a crown pattern, but we haven't finished it because we used some of the material to make cushion covers and you can't get that colour material any more. Just recently

RIRI TAIKA (TIGER LILY) *Tivaevae tataura*

# mareta MATAMUA

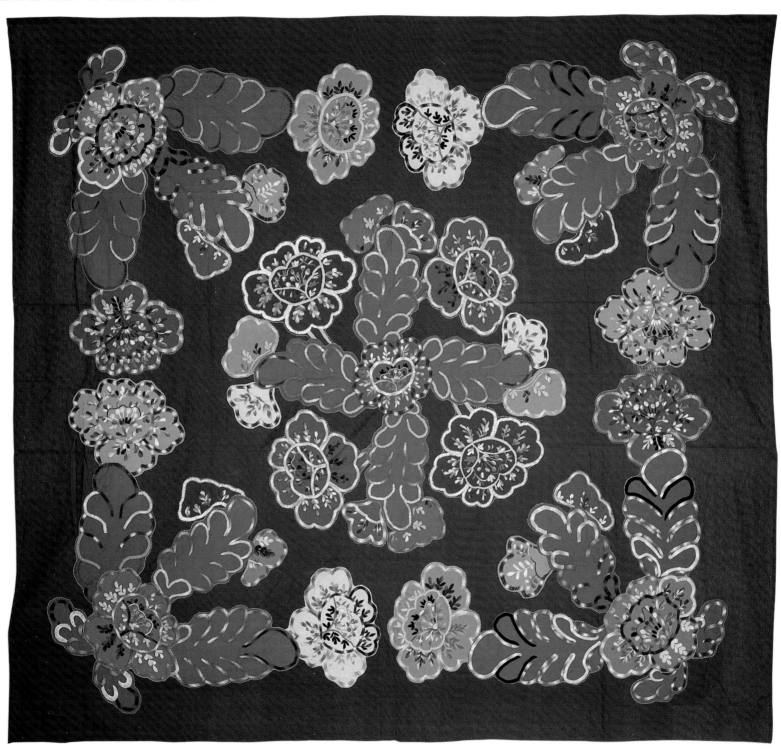

T I A R E  (FLOWERS)  *Tivaevae tataura*

we finished a tivaevae tataura, which was a flower pattern with embroidery on the flowers and leaves. We made the flowers and leaves out of azalin and sewed it onto a polyester mix sheet backing. When we washed it the flowers shrank, so we had to unpick the flowers —not the leaves—to take them off, iron them out and sew them back on. Maybe it shrank because of the different weight of the fabric. I don't really like using sheets to make tivaevae. I don't have any favorite patterns—I get my ideas from my mother and other women's tivaevae, and it gives me ideas for my own creations. I like using browns and creams, blues and greens on white; I usually like colours that other people don't like.

Vereara Maeva is a taunga, one of the best we've ever known. When you sit with her to sew a taorei, you have to be alert. When you ask her to design something the good thing about her is it's a one-off. Her tivaevae designs are never the same. I can't draw like Vereara. Her patterns are in her head and she can draw straight onto the fabric. I don't think I could make a taorei all by myself; it's much quicker when you work with a group. Our group has worked on a number of tivaevae together. Sometimes we've worked on until four in the morning to try and get

it right, and we've worked on a tivaevae taorei that took four years to complete.

My daughter Ani is just starting to sew tivaevae and has not finished her first one yet. Mum cut it for her. To cut a pattern we use a plastic mattress cover or those big plastic sheets. First you fold the material, then you put your pattern on the fabric, then draw it onto the material, cut it, open it out and tack it onto the backing sheet.

My granddaughter Nastashjia Cristell Katu is twelve years old and just started sewing last year. She is sewing a cushion cover. She went wrong with the one the teacher gave her at school and she came home and drew her own and started sewing it. When Mum tries to show her the correct way to sew, she still wants to sew it her way. Although she is learning to sew at school, my mother helps her. We encourage her to sew because that way she'll become interested in sewing tivaevae.

# MARETAMATAMUA

## ANI KATU

My Grandmother started teaching me how to sew simple stitches on a cushion cover when I was about seven years old. At the time we were living in Manihiki because my grandfather was the Government representative there. My grandmother and mother are always sewing, and it is normal for a daughter to carry on the tradition sewing tivaevae, cushion covers, pillowslips and tablecloths. As a teenager I was not keen on tivaevae making. I was forever moaning—the hours spent sewing and getting my fingers pricked or missing out on social-ising with my friends because I had to sit down to sew and learn a new stitch. My grandmother would say, 'When you get married, what are you going to cover your husband with' or 'What is your husband going to sleep on?' 'I'm not getting married', would be my reply to her.

Today I am glad that my grandmother has intro-duced me to the art of tivaevae making. I am sewing

*Four generations—Nastashjia, Mareta, Esther, Ani.*

a tivaevae with the tigerlily pattern by myself and it would be an accomplishment for me to finish, as it is the first one I have sewn without any help. I may not be an artist or a cutter yet, but I am planning to draw, cut and sew a tivaevae on my own and I hope that my grandmother will live to see what she has helped me to attain.

C R O W N  *Tivaevae taorei*

# NAPIER MITAERA

*I think I was about nine or eight years old when I started sewing. I loved sewing. I wanted to use my mother's sewing machine, but she wouldn't let me—it was a pedal one. So when my mother went out somewhere I'd rip up some of our old sheets, get on the machine and just do straight sewing, then my mother would come home and give me a hiding.*

We were really poor back then. My mother sewed our clothes, and I'd use all the waste bits to make patchwork cushions. In those days very few people had sewing machines. People would say, 'If you have a sewing machine in your house, you are a woman.' Until recently it was important for a girl to be skilful at sewing and cooking; her husband's status depended on it.

My mother used to sew all her bits of tivaevae taorei ready on one string. She knows how to count to make the pattern up. She would give me and my sisters a needle. One girl, one needle. She calls out, 'one blue' and you thread it on the needle, then 'light blue', 'two red' and we thread. Eight blocks for one whole tivaevae. My mother would start the pattern and we'd follow. My mother threaded all her bits ready on one string for sewing and I would try sewing it up, but it was all wrong. My mother would

# NAPIERMITAERA

say, 'Who's been on my tivaevae? You kids think this is for playing? You think this is a toy?' I liked playing with scissors, needles and cotton, and I would pick up my mother's embroidery and practise, but the moment my mother came home I'd run away. I used to think it was easy and that I could sew.

My father worked at the bakery and he would bring home all the cloth flour bags. The bags were still marked and we had no Janola, so my mother used to wash the bags with soap, sprinkle them with ashes from the umu and leave them to soak overnight. In the morning, no more marks. Us girls would undo the sewing thread of the bag and we'd keep that cotton to crochet. That's what we learned to crochet with. My mother can crochet and sew anything because she was taught by the nuns.

Out of the bags she'd make us dresses, slips and underpants. In those days, there was not elastic in the shops. We'd cut up the tyres from our bikes to make elastic for our pants and my mother crocheted the ends. I'd show them off at school. We'd have long pants down to our knees, and sometimes I'd swing around in my dress to make sure my pants could be seen and I'd

show off. I would get comments like, 'O naai i maani toou piripou?' [Who made your pants?]

My mother belonged to a vaine-tini group; it was like a working bee. You buy your material and then all get together to cut it out and sew it. Then you take your piece home to sew it together. The next week we would get together at one of our houses or a meeting house to cut the pattern out and sew it up. The person whose tivaevae was being made would cook some special kai. It would only take a day to sew the pieces together. One woman draws the pattern, and some-times we use each other's patterns. Sometimes a woman doesn't want to share her pattern.

When I'm working on my own I can sew one tivaevae a month. I don't know how to cut a tivaevae. I get my cousin or someone to cut it for me. I do my housework and in my spare time I sew. If I get visitors, I put down my tivaevae and chat. To me it's the sort of work you don't do regularly. When I feel like doing it, I do; when I don't feel like doing it, I don't. The thing is I have more spare time now. I'm alone here, I don't cook much and I have no family to look after. I just look after myself.

K A P E (TARO LEAVES) *Tivaevae tataura*

# TAURAARENGA MOUAURI

*I first started sewing when I was at school. I was about sixteen years old. Taorei was sewn and taught by the old mamas; tivaevae manu was introduced to the island much later. In about 1960, two women from Rarotonga came over and taught sewing to the ladies here on Mauke—Tepaeru Opo and Tepaeru Tereora. They taught us about sewing; that was when I first started to learn to sew tivaevae.*

I joined our vaine-tini group; there were about four women in a group to sew one tivaevae. We'd use about four yards of material. We would buy our own material and some of the women would share their designs with us. When we sewed a taorei, we'd follow someone's patterns, tear all the material about an inch square and thread the small squares onto a piece of cotton. We would all take a section of the tivaevae, sew our part and then bring them all back and sew them together to make up the tivaevae.

I prefer sewing tivaevae manu because a taorei takes a long time. I love red, blue, green and yellow, orange and pink, and I like sewing flowers.

You know us Maori, we give tivaevae away for presents at a marriage or a haircutting or something like that. I find it hard giving my tivaevae away. I've got nine children and I've given them all tivaevae.

KAUTE (HIBISCUS) *Tivaevae taorei*

# TOKERAU MUNRO

*I was about eighteen when I made my first tivaevae and I've still got it. Sewing tivaevae requires a lot of patience. Women who can design, sew and cut tivaevae are considered to have special skills and are called taunga. Not all women who sew and cut tivaevae are designers.*

My mother could sew, but she can't cut and design. I can design, cut and sew, and I've taught my daughters and daughter-in-law to cut and sew. We learn from our mothers, who learned from their mothers, and it's passed on from one generation to the next.

I was always interested in sewing when I was young. That's why I teach the girls how to sew while they are still young. When I left school and started working, I learned how to sew. I used to take my patchwork to my cousin for her to cut it, but later on she said, 'You can do it'. So I sat down and started learning to draw patterns and cut it out myself. Sometimes I'd get patterns from other people and alter them to my liking.

I enjoy working with women's groups. I'm a member of CIANGO (Cook Islands Non-Government Organisation) and NCW (National Council of

75

Women) and have co-ordinated the exhibitions for their conferences. In 2000 I went to the 7th Festival of Pacific Arts in New Caledonia with an exhibition of tivaevae. It was a wonderful experience, sharing with all the other participants from other countries. There was a lot of interest in our exhibition and we sold quite a lot of handicrafts.

There are about twenty women in my group. When we get together at different times we talk about work, our families and what we are going to sew for our next show. The women always come to me if they need help with their tivaevae and if they want me to cut one out for them. They'd choose their own material and I'd cut it. I don't mind teaching and helping them. In a big group sewing tivaevae doesn't take long—my group can finish two tivaevae in one week. For a tivaevae manu, we might cut it out one day, the next day spread the pattern onto the backing on the table, all helping with the tacking, then start sewing the same day.

For a tataura, if you had flowers in each corner and the center of each side of the tivaevae, each woman would take the flowers home to sew and I would sew the leaves, then we'd come back the following week to put it together. We'd spread it out on the table and help tack the finished pieces onto the backing.

Sewing tivaevae taorei is more complicated as it is made up of thousands of pieces of material the size of postage stamps and the designs are more like mosaic patterns. It takes more women to sew a taorei and can take anything from one to two years to finish.

When visitors come home I lay out my tivaevae on the beds. If it's just us, I don't bother. So much work has gone into it that I only use it for special occasions. Tivaevae is a most valuable article in the Cook Islands, treasured by the owners who find it very difficult to part with them.

R O T I (ROSE) *Tivaevae tataura*

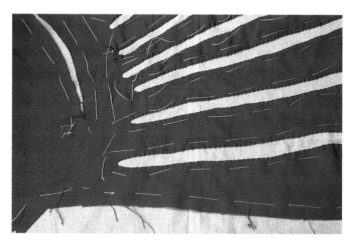

# GRACE NGAPUTA

*My mother designed, cut and sewed tivaevae and now I'm doing the same. I learned to sew from my mother —she was a planter. She looked after the family and then would go and work in the plantation. I'm a planter; I have a market in town. I've raised my family and also found time to design my patterns and sew tivaevae.*

An idea comes into my head and I just draw it. I sometimes take my sewing to the market and practise my stitches on a piece of material. One day a local man came to the market and I saw a pattern for tivaevae on his shirt. I asked him if I could borrow his shirt for a couple of days as I'd seen something in it. He gave me the shirt and I took it home and drew the part of the pattern I liked for a tivaevae.

When my mother sewed her tivaevae she would ask me to watch her. That's how I started to sew. She drew a pattern on a pillowslip, just something easy for me to sew—just plain sewing, like satin stitch, slip stitch and stem stitch. When that was finished she showed me a more difficult stitch. I sewed mainly pillowslips and cushions.

When I was about eighteen she showed me how to make a tivaevae. She would fold the material into four or eight pieces, depending on the pattern.

81

# GRACE NGAPUTA

She would draw the pattern of a flower or a leaf, like the matirita [chrysanthemum] or the riri [lily], onto the material and then cut out the pattern. We'd lay the backing sheet on the floor, put the cut-out pattern on top and then tack it to the material. After that she would tell me how to sew it.

In those days, thirty to forty years ago, they used to do plain sewing with very small stitches and fine cotton, not like the pearl cotton we sew with today, which is much thicker. We sewed the leaves and flowers with one kind of cotton.

The women of today sew their tivaevae with all colours of pearl cotton. It's nice when you look at it, but when you compare the tivaevae in the old days with the ones of today, I think the sewing in the old days was much neater.

I think that just a few women today take care and do neat sewing. They want to have neat sewing on their tivaevae. But some do it as quick as they can, just to say, 'I made a tivaevae'.

When I started sewing, my mother told me, 'When you sew you sew skilfully, so when people come to look at your sewing it is neat; then they will like it.' People look at the back of the tivaevae to check the stitches. Today I'm used to sewing the neat way. I have

MATIRITA (CHRYSANTHEMUM) *Tivaevae tataura*

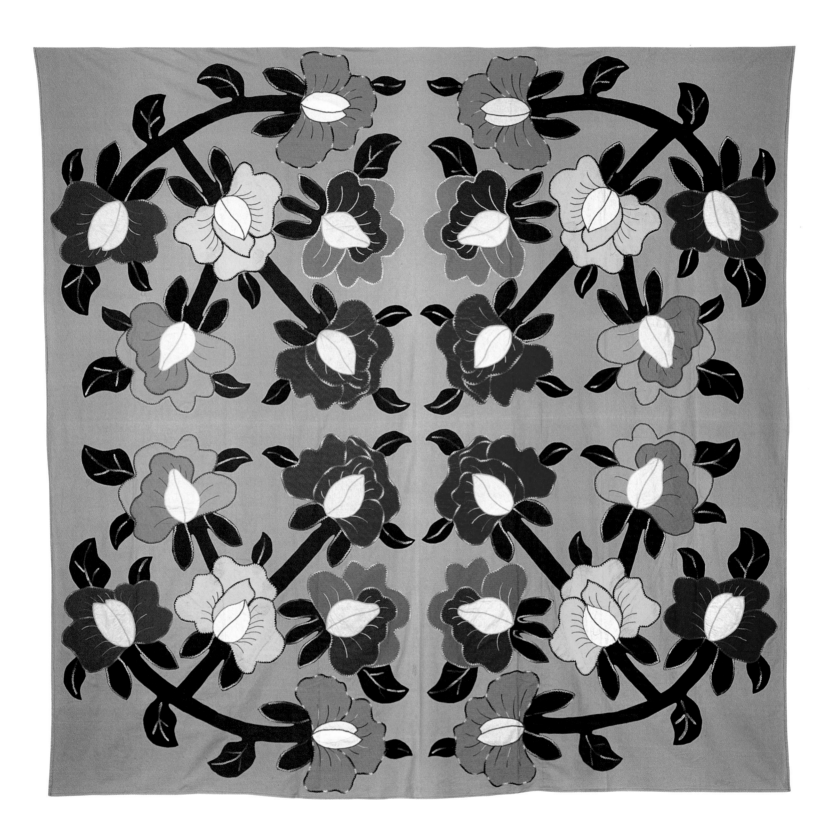

R O T I  (ROSE BUDS)  *Tivaevae tataura*

designed, cut and sewed a lot of tivaevae. I wish I had more time to be able to finish the tivaevae that I have cut.

Sometimes I join a vaine-tini group, but I usually work on my own. To my thinking, it's better to sew it yourself than to have a group of women sewing the same tivaevae because you look at the way you sew. It's neat, but another woman may not be so neat in her sewing. It's not the same. Some take long stitches, some take short stitches. You can see when many hands have sewn a tivaevae.

I used to take my tivaevae to the women's display in Avarua and I have won prizes. Some people bring the same old tivaevae that's been sitting in their glory box for so many years to the show. It's better to make a new one for each show instead of bringing the old one. Some ladies make new tivaevae every year, some don't. These days I might not take a tivaevae to the show because I haven't finished any new ones. It takes a long time if you want to make a nice tivaevae. It takes me two to three years to make a tivaevae if I've

got a nice one with hard stitches because I want to make the sewing neat.

I don't like to show anyone my patterns until I've finished sewing the tivaevae. After that I don't mind women copying. I feel proud. I think when you share like that it helps you to get new ideas for yourself.

I mainly make tivaevae manu and tataura now. Some women used to embroider their work straight onto the backing. These days women do their embroidery first and then sew it onto the backing—they say it's easier.

I have raised six children and I have sewn tivaevae for them. When my daughters were married we decorated around the main tables with tivaevae. When my son had his haircutting ceremony I put a tivaevae on his chair.

86

TARO LEAVES AND CRABS *Tivaevae manu*

RIRI IOTEPA (CHRISTMAS LILY) *Tivaevae manu*

# TARANGATAUA

*I was born on Rarotonga of Aitutakian parents. I've lived all my life in Aitutaki and I have eleven children. I work as a cook for a hotel and I look after my grandchildren.*

My mother died when I was very young and my grandmother raised me. My grandmother told me that my mother was one of the best sewers on the island. Maybe I've followed her ways. I'm the only one in my family who sews.

I taught myself to sew. When I was about 14, I used to sit and watch my aunty's way of cutting and sewing. When she put her sewing down I would pick it up and start sewing. She would smack me and hide her sewing and thread away.

At about 16, I asked my grandmother to buy me some material and thread and that's when I learned how to sew. My first piece of sewing was a pillowcase.

I went to Rarotonga when I was about eighteen to stay with my aunty, Teina Ngataua. I watched how she folded the material and cut the tivaevae out.

When I came back to Aitutaki, I asked my grandmother if she would buy some material, but she was worried that I would waste it. So the next time I went back to Rarotonga I cut out a tivaevae in front of my aunty and she said to me that I was more clever than her. So, since then, I've been designing and cutting tivavevae for myself and for other women.

My first tivaevae wasn't very nice but the more I cut, the better I got. I'm still cutting. I think I've cut over a hundred tivaevae I can't remember, there's been too many.

I cut and design for other women—they tell me what they want and I'll cut. I'm lucky I don't need to ask anyone to do my tivaevae. I am very happy that I know how to sew and cut. I just draw and cut whatever comes into my head. I can draw anything—I've just finished cutting a peacock for a lady.

I sew tivaevae for my children or if there's a wedding and I sew for the tutaka. I have a special feeling when I give one to a friend or my children.

I have seven boys and four girls and I've tried to teach my daughters. It's been hard going to work, looking after my family and cutting and sewing tivaevae.

PEACOCK AND GRAPES *Tivaevae tataura*

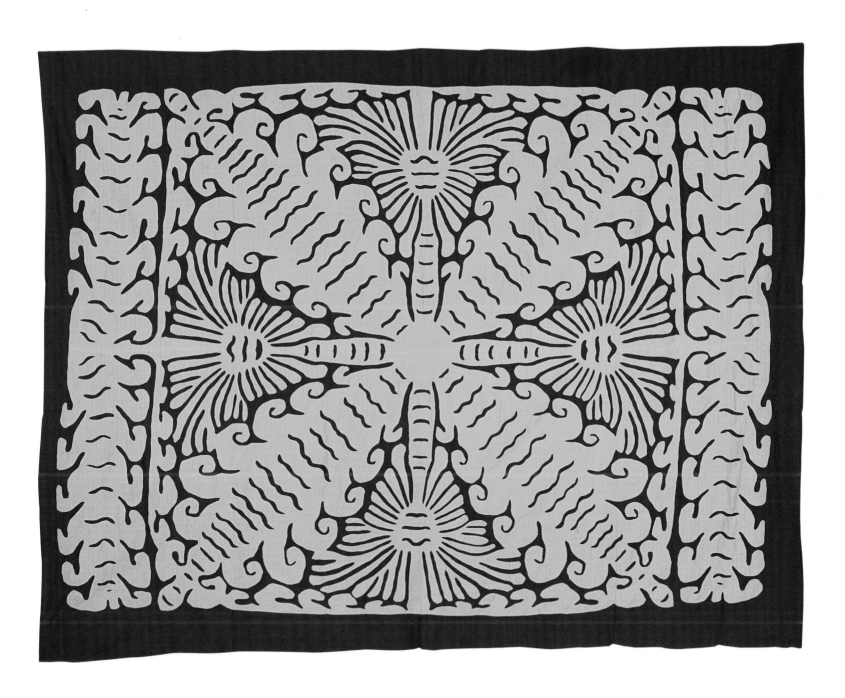

S E A   U R C H I N S   *Tïvaevae manu*

# TITINUMANGA

*My mother used to sew tivaevae taorei. In those days we didn't really treasure the tivaevae, we'd use them and wash them. I started sewing tivaevae when I was about eighteen. I used to watch the old mamas sewing and practise myself. I once saw a tivaevae taorei of my mother's—she died when I was about twelve.*

I used to teach needlework and I would take my sewing to school. During the break I would sew and talk. An elderly European woman used to hold afternoon classes and she taught us embroidery and showed us books with different patterns.

When I got married, I took with me eleven tivaevae which I had made myself. In those days women stayed home and cleaned the house, worked in the garden and looked after the children. The men would go planting and fishing. I remember joining a vainetini group in Titikaveka in the 1930s. There were about eight women in the group and we would sew about two tivaevae manu a week. I sewed tivaevae manu in a group, but the coloured ones, the tivaevae tataura, I worked on by myself. Sometimes a tere party from Tahiti would visit and the Tahitian women would bring their tivaevae and share their patterns with us.

93

# TITINUMANGA

*The sewing on the underside is often so neat that the tivaevae could be used in reverse*

Most women joined vaine-tini groups as there were no jobs. We would get together at the meeting house or one of the ladies' homes in the afternoon and do needlework and sew tivaevae. When we finished our work at home we would come together at the local meeting house with our lunch and talk and sew. We sung utu and imene tuki [church songs] while we sewed. Then we would go home to cook tea. Sometimes at night after our evening meal we'd go back to the meeting house and sew by kerosene and benzene lamps. There were no electric lights.

We mainly used two colours—red and white. We would each put in so much money to buy the material. It cost about two shillings and sixpence a yard. The material was much thicker than today's material.

ZINNIA *Tivaevae tataura*

# TITINUMANGA

I love sewing tivaevae tataura. When I sew tivaevae tataura I do my embroidery straight onto the backing. I enjoy needlework and trying out different stitches. I've noticed some of the work today doesn't lie flat. My daughters sew tivaevae but they are not keen; they'd rather buy their bedspreads from the shop—maybe it's because they've got to go to work. I've been trying to get my grandchildren interested but they're not keen either. My eyes are not good. I feel I'm not really interested now—I've made so many tivaevae, over a hundred. I've given them to special friends, my children, grandchildren, for weddings, birthdays. I sometimes wonder if I've wasted my time sewing. I feel that people don't really treasure them. Each one was special to me and I had special feelings about each one. If I sewed every day it would take me about three months to make one tivaevae. Some of my tivaevae I've got have faded because they've been packed in the box too long. Most of my patterns are of flowers; I love flowers and gardening.

My granddaughter asked me to sew her a tivaevae. I think I'm getting too old and I don't feel the same way about my sewing as I used to. It's getting too much work. I've just finished this one for my last grandson for his wedding and I think it may be my last one, I don't know.

POINSETTIAS *Tivaevae tataura*

# TEPAERU OPO

*I started sewing when I was sixteen. My grandmother, mother and aunties all sewed. I remember my mother used to sew our clothes. She tried to make things easier for me. She taught me how to sew and weave. Sometimes I'd go crooked so she'd come along and fix it up, but she always praised my work no matter what. That would make me try harder.*

There was no elastic in those days, so when she sewed our pants, my mother, like some of the mamas, would use strips of kiriau and pandanus. But they didn't know how to tie a good knot and the children would tie a square knot in the kiriau which was very hard to undo. When they came to do their business, they couldn't get the knot undone and they'd have to snap it which meant they then didn't have anything to hold their pants up. Then they'd use the rubber from the bike tyres as elastic.

I was employed by Internal Affairs, with Tepaeru Tereora, to train and work with women's groups here on Rarotonga and on the outer islands. We went to the outer islands and taught the women sewing, embroidery, crochet, cooking and how to be self-sufficient. The women in the outer islands cooked over an open fire and we taught them how to make a smokeless stove. We had the plans, the moulds and the measurement of concrete and sand. The only thing that discouraged the women from making the stove was the need for a good stand to place the stove on so that you could stand up and cook without bending down.

We would tell the ladies to ask their papas to make a stand, but you know what papas are like, they look down on what the women want to do and they're not very helpful. In the end though, they did enjoy the results—nice tasty food.

I've taught my daughters to sew tivaevae and I'm involved with women's activities, that's why I'm a member of the National Council of Women. I'm always happy to work with the women, to teach and share my skills.

99

100

R I R I   T A I K A   (TIGER LILY)   *Tivaevae tataura*

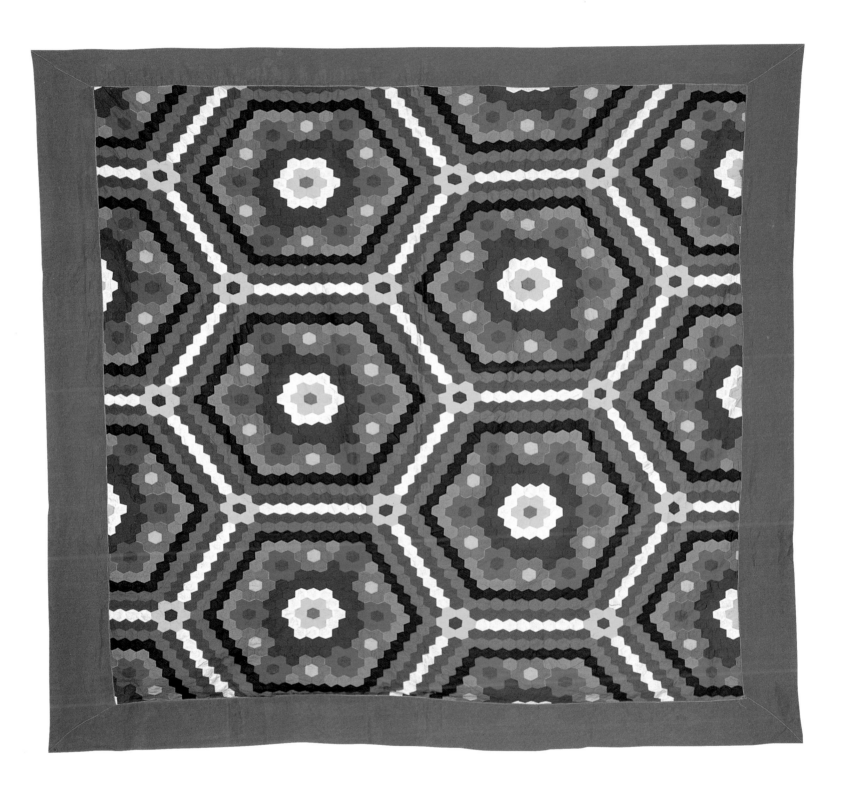

PAKA ONU (TURTLE BACK) *Tivaevae manu*

# VAINE PAPA

*As a teenager I used to draw patterns on pieces of paper and cut them out. I didn't start sewing tivaevae until much later. A papaa lady named Helen McCarthy taught me a lot of things; she taught me how to cut a pattern out and to sew different embroidery stitches and crochet.*

I worked as a nurse full time and in my spare time I would go to Helen and learn more. I started embroidering pillowcases, tablecloths and cushions before I started sewing tivaevae. I caught on by watching the lady next door cut and sew tivaevae, and when I asked her if she would teach me, she said no. My first tivaevae was a large hibiscus. I also learned how to sew from a couple of other women, Tepareru Opo and Tepaeru Terora, when they came to Mauke sometime in the 60s and taught us how to do needlework and cut and sew tivaevae. At about that time I also belonged to a Busy Bees Club, which was made up of mamas who worked for Government and would get together at the end of the day to sew.

I have faith in my work and the patterns I draw and cut. I get some of my ideas for patterns from dreams and by looking at other tivaevae and changing the pattern to make it look different. I got the idea for a pattern for one of my tivaevae from a lily

that was on a Christmas card. I spent a lot of time looking at the Christmas card then I changed it around until I got the pattern I liked. I like flowers— orchids, hibiscus and lilies—and I prefer to use dark colours. I sew in my spare time at night and after working hours. I give my tivaevae to special friends and, of course, my family.

I have a Young Women's Club here on Mauke where I teach young women who want to learn how to cut and sew tivaevae, cushion covers and pillowcases. I love making tivaevae and sometimes I design and can cut up to four tivaevae a day for different women. I prefer they ask me to cut their tivaevae rather than them copying my designs.

I was born in Mauke and have lived here all of my life. I've had five children, four boys and a girl, and they've all left here and are now living overseas. My daughter and I use to sew tivaevae together until she went to live in New Zealand.

TIARE MAORI (MAORI FLOWER) *Tivaevae manu*

*Tivaevae tataura—I got the idea from a lily that was on a Christmas card*

# PENRHYN
# NGATOKORIMARASMUSSEN

*I was born Ngatokorima but as a child growing up in Titikaveka I was known as Tiaoti (or Georgina). I started sewing tivaevae at the age of twelve because my elder sister Tu'anga and her family lived with us. In those days when you got married you would live with your parents until the fourth child.*

I would look after her kids. Being a young mother who was interested in sewing tivaevae, she had joined a vaine-tini group that I also joined when I grew into womanhood. My sister would bring her tivaevae home after her vaine-tini meetings and show me how to sew. I would help her with her tivaevae manu, tataura and taorei.

There were thirteen in my family—six girls and seven boys. All the girls could sew tivaevae. My mother could also sew tivaevae; a mother's role was to sew tivaevae for the boys, and the girls would have to sew for themselves. It's funny my Mum never gave me any tivaevae. She sewed and gave her ones to her sons, especially my brother Kairoa. In a way she wasn't really interested in sewing; she preferred cooking umu (earthoven) food and sitting by the fire keeping our pots full of food!

When I married my husband, Joe, I had no tivaevae. He had a glory box that was filled with a taorei, a

manu and a pair of embroidered pillowcases that his mother had made for him, so that encouraged me to make one for myself. In 1949, after saving up money from my paid job as a housegirl for the postmaster in town, I remember asking my mother (Koringo Mata Atua) to take my material to a Tahitian lady who lived in Ngatangiia (Nia Rua's wife) to cut one out for me so that I could sew it by myself. When I finished it in 1950, my father died and the tivaevae went with my dad in his grave.

My second tivaevae I made in Penrhyn. My mother-in-law, Mama Rongo, showed me some of her patterns. When I asked her where she got her patterns, she said from Tahiti. She cut a 'kiss me' flower pattern tivaevae manu. Mama Rongo didn't teach me but I was very good at drawing at school and I'm good at copying patterns, and that's how I learned how to cut tivaevae. If I copy a pattern I use different colours. I love using the colour green, I like green on green, purple on purple, I love dark colours that don't show the dirt – I don't put white in my taorei. With some materials the dye runs if you wash it. I look around my house and garden for ideas.

My first taorei was a lily pattern. I sewed by myself with Joe (my husband) helping me thread the squares.

*Tivaevae taorei—my first tivaevae was a lily pattern*

FLOWER BOUQUET  *Tivaevae taorei*

When I'd finished it I shared the pattern out to the sewing group (there were eight of us). Eight corners make a taorei with each of us sewing seventy-two lines each.

Our sewing group never came together every day to sew; instead we'd meet once, then share it out and each woman would take her sewing home and then whoever the tivaevae belongs to picks it up to sew all the pieces together. I love sewing taorei in a group. I used to sew when I'd finished my work and baby was asleep. I suppose I sewed taorei because my mother told me that taorei is for life, you will it from one generation to the next, and it is only used or put out on special occasions so it has a longer life than say the manu or tataura. It means that bit extra more to me when I pass it from my generation to my daughters and sons and they can pass it on to their children and so forth. I look after my tivaevae. I might put it on the bed for a week, then take it off the bed and hang it out on the line in the sun, pack it in a plastic bag and put it in the glory box. I have tivaevae on my husband and son's bed, but I never used to. I have to laugh when it got cold and he'd say, 'Where's the tivaevae? It should be on the bed, not in the box'. I think of my mother and what she used to say: 'Don't leave it in the glory box and bring it out when your husband dies. It's for your husband and sons to use now.' I don't like to see tivaevae that I've made left lying around, it makes me want to cry—but when you give it to someone you can't tell them how to look after it. They might come back and say, 'Well you gave it to me, why do you come back telling me how to look after it!'

I've had ten children and sewed tivaevae taorei, manu and tataura for all my sons and daughters. Some have died and have taken their share. Some of my sons have got seven tivaevae each. I've given tivaevae away for happy occasions like weddings for a couple of friends and my niece, but I sew and give them mainly to my own children and grandchildren; when I give my taorei to them, they know it's for life.

I'm seventy-one this year. If I add up the tivaevae I've sewn it's over seventy. And I've cut many many tivaevae for women who have wanted a manu or tataura and have helped women to sew their tivaevae.

I laugh at my daughter Vaine who is taking an interest now. I've cut three manu for her. But I'll let her tell her story.

112

## VAINE-IRIANO WICHMAN
### (NEE RASMUSSEN)

I can remember being ten and my Mum throwing me a pillowcase with hibiscus flowers for me to try my hand embroidering it with chain stitches. It wouldn't be until I was in my late twenties that I went back to my mum to ask her to cut my first tivaevae. It was a tiare maori pattern which I finished all by myself. I then decided to try my own hand at cutting tivaevae. I cut a breadfruit pattern and a pattern of light blue maire leaves on a white backing. To this day my mum says she still can't see the maire in it! I like sewing

tivaevae manu. I like the rhythm of sewing either the hem, zigzag or buttonhole stitch. I guess you could say I enjoy the fact that each stitch is adding up to the beautiful end result that is hard to see when you have just started. But I look forward to the feelings as the tivaevae starts to take shape, and then after it's completed it's like an achievement for me. Its almost like having a baby, isn't it?

Anyway, one day many moons gone now, I thought of my mum and wrote this about her.

### IN THE TIVAEVAE

*My mother sews her love into each stitch*
*That joins the tivaevae pattern*
*to the backbone*

*My mother is not educated*
*for money*
*Preferring to toil the soil*
*To feed our mouths*

*My mother knows the moons,*
*the tides, the seasons,*
*Planning her time between*
*Home and field.*

*Her parting words with each tivaevae distributed*
*Is 'I am with my children*
*whenever they sleep'.*

TIARE MAORI (GARDENIA) *Tivaevae manu*

*Tivaevae manu—blue maire leaves*

R A U   M I T I M I T I   O R O E N U A   (HORSE HEAD PLANT)   *Tivaevae manu*

116

# KIMIORASAMUEL

*Vereara Maeva showed me how to cut in the 1970s. I don't have any favourite patterns, just whatever comes into my mind. My favourite colours are green and blue. I used to work by myself, but then Vereara started a group. When she left I just sewed on my own until I started another vaine-tini group of women in the 1980s. I've given most of my tivaevae away as gifts for my friends and relatives. I use them in my house on the beds.*

MATARITA (CHRYSANTHEMUMS) *Tivaevae manu by Mary Daniel, also from Mangaia*

T A I R I I R I (FAN) *Tivaevae manu*

# PARAU TARUIA

*In my mother's family they all sewed. My grandmother Parengakaia designed and sewed some of the first taorei in the Cook Islands; they were very popular in those days. She had a women's group in Ngatangiia. Most of the women in the group were family and friends from within the village.*

My mother, Ruta Tixier, was a born artist, a very gifted woman and considered to be a taunga in her day. She could design, cut and sew tivaevae and didn't need a pattern. An idea would come into her head and she could draw freehand straight onto the fabric, and her designs were never the same. My Aunty Lafala would draw her designs for taorei onto a woven mat, like graph paper.

We went over to live in Manihiki in the 60s, and my mother and I taught the women there how to do embroidery, to make tivaevae tuitui tataura. Women in the northern group are well renowned for their fine weaving, but once they learned how to do embroidery they started to win prizes for their tivaevae tuitui tataura. We didn't teach them how to crochet, so instead of crocheting around the borders to join the pieces together, they would use lace.

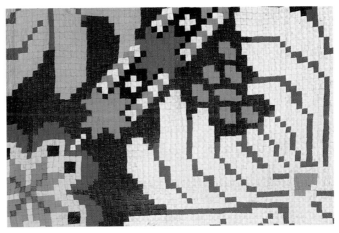

121

# PARAU TARUIA

I first learned how to sew when I was in grade seven at school. We learned simple embroidery stitches on sacking, and after that I mainly taught myself. When I started sewing tivaevae there was a Tahitian woman in Muri, who used to cut tivaevae for women who didn't know how to cut the patterns out themselves. My mother never kept copies of her designs, but I've tried to remember what I can in my own designs and add my own ideas to them. I'd say the more you do, the more creative you become. I love embroidery and I treasure all work. My mother designed one particular tivaevae, the cattleya orchid. She got the idea for this particular design when she saw the orchid while attending a conference in New Zealand. I did all the sewing and my daughter helped me with the blanket stitch around the border.

Over the years I've belonged to many women's groups and we've sewn tivaevae for exhibitions as well as for gifts for overseas visitors. In 1980 I represented the Cook Islands at the Festival of Pacific Arts in Papua New Guinea. On the way over to the festival we were on the same plane as the delegation from French Polynesia and the woman sitting next to me was telling me about a Cook Islands woman, Ruta Tixier, who had taught tivaevae making in Tahiti, and the Tahitian women were still using some of her designs. It was only after she'd told me her story that I told her it was my mother she was talking about. When they'd set up their display, the tivaevae taorei on display happened to be one of my mother's designs. At the 6th Festival of Arts on Rarotonga women from all around the island worked in groups, on different types of tivaevae for the festival exhibition. There were taorei, tataura, tuitui and manu. My group of women worked on the tivaevae tataura.

I love sewing and I feel sad that they don't teach young girls sewing in schools, like they did in the old days. They should introduce it back into the schools.

CATTLEYA ORCHID *Tivaevae tataura*

*Tivaevae taorei*

MIXED FLOWERS *Tivaevae tuitui tataura*

# TEINA TETUPUARIKI

*I taught myself sewing by watching the old mamas sew. As a child, my mother gave me pieces of cloth to make embroidered pillowcases and cushions as she felt that I was not quite ready to sew tivaevae. I sat for hours sewing and filling in the patterns I had drawn on the material. At times, I found using the same colour of thread boring so I'd use a different colour thread either for the leaves or another flower on the pattern.*

In between learning how to sew and growing up, I used to go hill climbing and picking fruit in the mountains with all the other kids. There was an abundance of wild guavas, berries and mangoes, and we used to fill our dresses with fruit before going home. But most times, when we'd get home, half the fruit would be squashed as we tripped and fell on the way down the hills. I tell you, it was really good fun.

As a young woman, I used to make my own dresses using my own patterns. I truly loved doing this and couldn't wait for my mother to give me pieces of material which our family friend on one of the trading ships used to bring home.

In one of my tivaevae taorei, I chose the spotted material that I thought would be nice as a tigerlily. I have sewn a wide border around it to make the pattern smaller. When I made this one, the beds were

*The beds were much wider—the old four-poster beds—and the tivaevae would hang down nicely on both sides of the bed*

# TEINA TETUPUARIKI

much wider—the old four-poster beds where you have mosquito netting hanging down from the canopy—and the tivaevae would hang down nicely on both sides of the bed. I love sewing fancy borders around my tivaeave and also love water lilies and flowers in my work. Another craze of mine is sewing butterflies beside the flowers.

In my younger days we used to sew in groups. We would go to one of the ladies' houses and she would cook a kaikai and we would sew and talk about what was happening around the island. This would be our gossip session and we'd sure hear a lot of news that way. In our sewing group, we would take turns doing each other's tivaevae. In other words, if it is my turn to have a tivaevae done, I choose and cut the

130

RIRI TAIKA (TIGER LILY) *Tivaevae taorei*

material and each lady is given the pattern to sew. They are given ample time to sew their portion and, after everyone's ready, the pieces are joined together to form a tivaevae. The beauty of this is that the tivaevae is finished quickly although it is a shame that the stitches are all different.

Until recently, it was important for a girl to be skilful in sewing because you could make nice things for your home. I design, cut and sew my own tivaevae and I enjoy sewing and listening to the radio. I have tried to get my granddaughter to take an interest in what I do but she has other interests. Girls today are very different from girls of yesterday. My only hope is that she will take care of all the embroidery and tivaevae that will one day be hers.

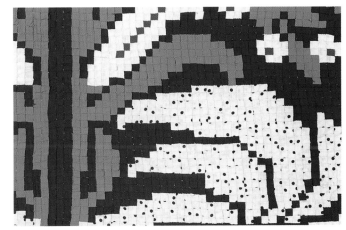

*I chose the spotted material that I thought would be nice as a tiger lily*

131

# E RERE

*E rere e taku tavake*
*Kua anga taau moe e rere*
*E apai atu koe ki Havaiki*
*te korero o teia kainga*
*te rongo o taku tivaevae*
*Me kura te rangi i te aiai*
*Ka maara au ia koe*

*Fly my tropical bird*
*Your sleeping is done so fly*
*Take with you to Havaiki*
*the stories of our home*
*the fame of my tivaevae*
*when the sky turns red*
*I will remember you*

KAURAKA KAURAKA
AUGUST 1990